THE ENTREPRENEURS GUIDE TO BUSINESS CREDIT

7 Steps to Access More Cash & Maximize Your Profits

MICA COLEMAN

DISCLAIMER

Healthy Financial Futures, Inc. cannot be responsible for errors in the preparation of the materials, nor the presentation of the material. You are advised that this book is presented to educate, empower and expand your knowledge in understanding business credit. For specific advice, prior to taking any action, consult with a business credit specialist, attorney, and accountant, of your selection. This book is for educational purposes only, and neither Healthy Financial Futures, Inc. nor its consultants are offering legal advice or other professional tax advice, in any fashion. Every vendor has its own credit policies and they are subject to change at any time.

All rights reserved. No part of this manual may be reproduced in any form or by any means without express written permission of the publisher. Violators will be prosecuted to the full extent of the law.

ENTREPRNUERS GUIDE TO BUILDING BUSINESS CREDIT

The Small Business Administration estimates that the lack of capital is one of the top reasons small businesses fail and most entrepreneurs' have unmanageable debt.

Healthy Financial Futures, Inc. has a system that will walk you step-by-step on how to build business credit and strengthen the results of building your business credit score. Your company can get unlimited amounts of business credit; but in order to obtain unlimited amounts of business credit and cash there are a few things you should know.

We highly recommend you read this book in its entirety first. As a real estate investor, business owner or entrepreneur this manual will give you a better understanding for the credit building process from the beginning to the end. After you have read this manual once, simply follow the step-by-step checklist on "How To Obtain Unlimited Business Credit" on our website healthyfinancialfutures.com and follow the process to financing your business future.

Most business failures are caused not by a shortage of good ideas or know how but by a lack of operating capital. Using the techniques in this guide, you can safely build a business credit history separate from your personal credit.

We've outlined all the necessary steps you need to completely be successful in building your business credit profile. There are many variables that can arise during your credit-building process so you must have patience. Remember good things come to those who wait. The good thing is if you are reading this manual and you follow the steps to setting up your business properly you won't have to wait too long to see the gold at the end of the rainbow.

Please visit us at

www.facebook.com/healthyfinancialfutres

for daily tips and answers to questions you may have. By the way don't forget to press the Like Button.

Table of Contents

#1 Why Building Business Credit Is Important 9

#2 Dealing With Lenders 22

#3 The Business Credit Bureaus 30

#4 Requirements for Building Business Credit 39

#5 Maintaining Your D&B Report 48

#6 How To Raise Your PAYDEX Score 52

#7 Find Out Who is Reporting On Your Business 60

Bonus Chapter Vendors For Building Your Business Credit Today 67

#1

Why Building Business Credit Is Important

Most entrepreneurs and small business owners have been in business for years, and don't realize that business credit even exists ... or how to establish a business credit file. It never seems to amaze me how many small business owners are running a business but aren't set up as a business. I estimate 90% of entrepreneurs have no idea what is business credit. I have been to several networking events and when I tell people what I do most people have heard about business credit but really don't understand the value and the process of building a business credit profile.

Every business owner or entrepreneur should ask themselves the following questions:

- ✓ Have I ever been declined for a business loan or financing?
- ✓ Have I went to my local bank as the first

place to apply for a loan?
- ✓ Could I use a business line of credit for working capital?
- ✓ Do I need, now or in the future, to lease equipment or purchase products?
- ✓ Am I getting the cash flow I need with what I am currently doing?
- ✓ Can I obtain easy, fast approval on credit cards for my business?
- ✓ Do I currently receive the most favorable credit terms from vendors?
- ✓ Is my personal credit maxed out; which limits me to get financing for my business?

If any of these questions apply to you and you have more "yes" then "no" answers? Then that means you haven't built your business credit profile properly. More importantly you haven't been educated properly on how to build a business profile separate from your personal credit profile.

Unfortunately when most individuals go into business; especially entrepreneurs, they never stop to think about the total cost and liability they may carry personally. Most of the time when small business owners like myself think of starting a business the first place you look for money is within your personal assets. No one ever thinks to build a foundation for his or her business prior to starting a business. If you're thinking about starting a business or have been in business the best thing you can do for yourself and your business is building a business credit profile.

One of the keys to building business credit is

knowing your financial foundation as it stands today. Do you know?

You must have an idea or a potential outlay of profits before going to any funding source. It is important to have your financial blue print in place before you apply. If you don't have your financial blue print in place you are completely wasting your time.

If you are savvy and know the amount of capitol that goes into a business and the leveraging power of having business credit prior to starting a business you are part of the 10% of entrepreneurs that make it in the first 5 years of building your business.

But often times owners don't know where to go and get the capitol to actually start the business without using their personal finances, friends, and family.

The lack of useful information available on how to finance your business is very limited; especially when it comes to building business credit; which is not widely accessible.

This book will help you understand how to finance, operate and expand without putting your personal finances, or your family's future, in jeopardy.

Before you even apply for credit we suggest you visit our website and make sure your business is in compliance. You can go to healthyfinancialfutures.com where you can get a free consult on building your business credit NOW !!!

If your business passes our 20-point compliance checklist; which meets most lenders creditability standards your business can go straight to funding.

However; if you're like most small businesses you may not meet the criteria of most banks or alternate lenders. Why? Because you haven't established anything in your actual business name.

When you apply for credit for a business, most creditors will pull your business credit report. This credit might have been used for anything in your business name ... from credit cards ... to loans ... to equipment.

So what happens if they pull your business credit report and there's nothing there? The bank or any type of lender will rely on your personal credit to guarantee your request. If there's no business credit file, they're not able to lend credit to your business. One of the main reasons you need a business credit report is the ability to receive more funding and cash credit in your business name.

Here's another reason why you need to build business credit: to save money!

This is the most important reason. Building business credit can save yourself and your business money. How many times have you, as an entrepreneur, worked a full time job to fund your business dream? Yep, that's right most entrepreneurs are trading their time for money in hopes to one day go off on their own to have their own business. I think that is great for those who can do that. But I have seen it so many times where a person's job gets in the way of their entrepreneurial dream. Reality is the comfort of a consistent pay check clouds the judgment of even thinking outside the box to create or even replace a full time job income. This is where I say building a foundation a.k.a "Business credit" can eventually replace your income if you structure your business right.

By having a business credit profile you won't increase your personal debt with business matters. It will help your business for many reasons (expansion, products, payroll, equipment, etc).

Building a strong business credit rating is vitally important to your success; not only will you save your personal assets you can get lower interest rates on loans and credit cards. Without it, you'll pay much more (in higher interest rates) for the money you borrow ... if you can borrow at all. In fact, banks – which say they want to help small business owners – actually turn down over 97% of all business loan applications. They don't make it easy! It never seems to amaze me how many small businesses go to a bank FIRST to seek capital for their business when the bank is the last place you want to ask for money unless you have been in business for a minimum of 5 years or more. So if you're a start up business and looking for capital; please read this book very carefully and follow the steps as well as the checklist on our website at healthyfinancialfutures.com.

So if you're a start up and your trying to get funding for your new business. The difference from you borrowing money versus your business is discussed in this scenario below. How does this work? Here's an example:

Let's say you need $50,000 for a piece of equipment or for products. Without a strong business credit rating, your bank will use your personal credit only. If you get approved, you'll have in this example an interest rate of 18%; if you don't have the best credit. With a D&B

(Dunn & Bradstreet) report, you can lower your rate to perhaps 10% and you don't have to guarantee the loan with your personal assets.

Here's a quick comparison:

	Personal Loan	Business Loan
Loan Amt:	$50,000	$50,000
Interest Rate:	18%	10%
Lease Term:	60 months	60 months
Monthly Payment:	$1,269.67	$1,062.35
Total Payments:	$76,180.20	$63,741.00

Total Savings: $12,439.20

By simply building business credit and setting up your business properly you can save yourself thousands of dollars! When it comes to the bottom line, you have to understand the leveraging power of business credit as a business owner.

The truth is ... you don't really have a business credit rating until you start building one!

When I first started out building business credit I had no clue what to do or where to start. All I knew was to apply for credit in my business name. And guess what? The first place I went was my local bank. At that time I didn't know any better. However; luckily for me I was properly structured and compliant to get funding from my local bank. However: I didn't know how to continuously build my business credit and what type of credit to apply for. So what do you do when you don't know? It's like throwing a dart in the dark in hopes to get the bull's eye. And if you're like myself being an entrepreneur we wear a lot of hats so we don't have time to play the guessing game. That game is not fun when your trying to accomplish your goals and access capitol to expand. So my mission is to make your process as simple as possible through educating you on what is needed and how to start applying for simple cards before your company start tackling the big conservative lenders.

#2

Dealing With Lenders

I will never understand as an entrepreneur why we always consider the "Bank" as our first lending source. If you learn anything from this guide the Bank is the last place you want to go, especially if you're a start up. We automatically think just because we have been banking at a particular institution for a long period of time that as a new business owner the bank should give you money. Right?.......Wrong just like every place you go to get any type of financing there are guidelines. Unfortunately, most bank guidelines aren't created for new businesses or start-ups.

If you have been in business for ... 1 year ... 5 years ... or 20 years, it doesn't matter. Any bank or lenders main concern is your business credit rating. If you don't have a business credit rating any type of lender will consider your loan a personal loan (with personal guarantees), which means you're liable for ALL the debt owed!

Every lender has approval guidelines they follow when considering your loan application. There are several things they review and examine. To give you some of the basic standards of qualifying with most lenders are as follows:

Your business should have:

- 411 national directory assistance listing
- Bank account with a balance
- You must have at least 5 trade credits accounts reporting to credit bureaus ...
- A Duns Number
- Pay Dex Score must be at least 75 or higher
- Debt coverage ratio of 5:1 or better

These are some of the things that are needed and if one item is unfavorable, your banker may turn against you! So is receiving funding easy? Yes and No. "Yes" if you have all your ducts in a row. "No" if you don't. Also it is very important that you set up your business properly from the beginning so that your financial funding foundation is strong.

At Healthy Financial Futures, Inc. that is our mission to build your company a strong business credit foundation. Before I had the knowledge that I have today I thought I had everything in place. For example, I had my corporation, EIN#, bank account, trade lines, etc. Well guess what? I was denied funding on something so simple I could of kicked myself. I was denied because my address was not reporting the same on all documents. That's why I can't stress enough about building your business properly all the way down to the minor detail, such as a Suite # Vs. #7 as an example. Make sure everything matches so there are no questions.

So how easy can any small business receive funding when they have to produce documentation such as the following?

- Interim financial statements
- Most-recent Federal Tax Returns for each principal owner
- Accountant-prepared financial statements including Profit & Loss statement and Balance Sheet for the last 3 years
- Personal financial statements for each principal owner
- Organization papers, such as incorporation papers, DBA papers, business licenses, etc.

- List of business and personal assets that can be used as collateral
- Names and contact information for at least three credit references

These few things can get you turned down; but they can also get you a whole lot of cash. Now I know what you are asking...... what if I am just starting out? These documents can be very difficult for a start-up business to supply ... especially if they've never done any business before. Many "banks" expect a business to be already established before they request financing ... but you can get started without it! Like I said before –the bank is the last place to go for a start-up.

If you are looking to get $30,000 or less there are lenders who don't require all the items previously listed. Speaking from experience I have worked with several lenders that requested the following items below and I received $50,000 line of credit for my business.

- Articles Of Incorporation
- Statement of Information
- Business License
- Current Business Bank Account with that Bank

Now most alternate lenders will lend you money just for having a business account, merchant account or just being structured properly. I always suggest the first thing any small business owner or entrepreneur should do is open an account in their business name. Opening a bank account in your business name helps you out in taxes, lending, and longevity. It is also a strong indicator of when you actually started your business. The longer you have had a business account open in your business name the better. Please make sure when you are opening up the business account that you are opening the account in a separate social security number also known as an EIN# (Employer Identification Number). You never want to open your business account with your personal social security number because the whole idea of building business credit is building credit separate from your personal credit.

Subscribe to Our YouTube Station and we have an instructional on how to get your own separate EIN#(Employer Identification Number) for your business.

#3

The Business Credit Bureaus

For many years, great companies have been declined by banks because of incorrect information on their business credit report … or, as in most cases, because they don't have a business credit report at all. You may be wondering if you even have a business credit report. If you don't know, then you most likely don't have one! However; if you have started building your business credit and have just about everything on our 20 point compliance checklist, your in good shape.

> GO TO Experian.com click on Business Credit Scores. Type in your business name and see if your business has its own credit report

There are three major companies that collect business information and publish it. They are as follow:

- Dun & Bradstreet,
- Experian,
- Business Equifax.

Dun & Bradstreet (D&B) is the largest business credit reporting bureau with over 75% of the business credit reporting market. The website offers user-friendly tools for the business owner to check for their business listing and feedback from the clients and customers. But the other two are catching up quickly. Most lending institutions incorporate the information, and use the commercial scoring model, that they retrieve from Dunn & Bradstreet database. This is internationally used for all businesses; especially in the import and export business.

To help you understand the business credit

bureaus a little better I will give you a brief introduction on the history of business credit bureaus.

Dun & Bradstreet (D&B) started back in the 1800's and has been collecting business information for over 150 years. They compile the information that business owners provide them and then sell it to other companies. The most important thing for you to know is that they are the largest and most predominant business credit bureau in the marketplace. I have interviewed several banks and the #1 place most banking institutions check is D&B. So it would be advantageous to have a D&B number so your business can be a part of that market place.

A little side bar information- if you try to obtain a D&B number don't be fooled by their sales people. You can get a D&B number for FREE. Yes I said that correctly. FREE !!! Most individuals when they try to build business credit by their self they run into a lot of sales pitches and end up paying a lot of money that will lead them down a brick wall of more debt and no financing. Trust me I've been there and seen it all; that's why my mission is to educate entrepreneurs like myself to build business credit the smart and simple way.

Steps to take to obtain your D&B credit number for free

1. Go to http://www.dnb.com
2. Look near the top right side and click on "D-U-N-S Number"
3. Click "Get D-U-N-S".
4. Go to the bottom right side of the page,

then, click on the icon "Get a FREE DUNS Number".

5. Once the form is complete you will either get an email with your e-update password and Duns number.
6. If you get an email stating that the information is not accurate, give D&B a call to update your business information.

Recently, other companies have entered the business credit world as well.

Experian, who you may already be aware of because it is also used as a personal credit bureau, now has a business division called Corporate Experian. Several lenders now base their lending decisions on Corporate Experian instead of D&B.

Equifax, which is also known in the personal

credit bureau, is also entering the business credit world and they are offering an extensive business credit report.

There are a few others, but they're not big players and you won't need to worry too much about them. These include PayNet, FDInsight, BusinessCreditUSA, and ClientChecker.

Business credit is not like your personal credit wherein, when you turned 18 and got your first credit card, you immediately had a credit report. In order to set up your business credit profile you need to file with Dun & Bradstreet. Once your business files with D&B you'll be given a D&B number, or what is also known as a DUNS number.

Lenders will ask you for this number ... and they use it to access your credit rating. Here is a very important fact that I cannot stress enough:

"You must follow the steps of setting up a proper business before you establish your D&B file."

We'll go into the details later, but there are prerequisites that you need to meet before you begin to set up a business credit file. You must know what to do ... the order to do these steps in ...and then manually set up a D&B credit file to ensure that the information is completely accurate.

It is very important that each step of this system is followed precisely. If one step is skipped or you don't complete one step before moving on, then you'll hinder the ability of your business to operate at maximum capacity. Most importantly you will jeopardize the amount of money to borrow if you don't follow the right steps; which will result in you having to use your personal credit report to qualify for loans. And my goal is to educate and empower you so you don't use your personal finances to build your business.

#4

Requirements for Building Business Credit

First, let me clarify one thing: You're not a business unless you are incorporated or a limited liability company, but you might be "in business". You must be a corporation S or C-Corp, LLP or an LLC in order to build true business credit. If you aren't, you won't be able to separate your personal credit from your business credit. If you don't have a separate business entity, that is the first step to starting a business; although you may already be in business.

It is very important to know what type of corporation you are forming in regards to limiting your personal liability while operating a business. It's best to weigh the pros and cons when deciding which entity to form. I will give you a brief description of each type of entity; however it is very imperative that you seek a tax advisor before structuring your corporate structure.

Limited Liability Corporation (L.L.C.)

Limited personal liability of owners; unlimited number of owners; owners pay taxes based on their share of ownership; requires filing of Articles of Organization with the Secretary of State.

Limited Liability Partnership (L.L.P.)

Similar to the L.L.C., but designed for professional organizations such as CPAs and attorneys; requires filing of Articles of Organization with the Secretary of State. A Limited Partnership consists of at least one general partner and other limited partner or a general partner is personally liable for the partnership's debts; limited partners are not personally liable, as long as they do not materially participate in the partnership's management; partners are taxed based on ownership percentages; requires filing a Partnership Registration with the Secretary of State. Once you have chosen how you will operate, you need to file your Articles of Incorporation, Articles of Organization, Partnership Agreement or "Doing Business As" with your Secretary of State or your respective Secretary of State. The cost to file will vary by state.

S-Corporation

An S-Corporation is a corporation for all purposes except for taxes. An S corporation generally offers liability protection to its owners (shareholders) and is a conduit where the profits or losses of the S corporation flow through to the shareholders, partners, or members. Liability of the owners for debts and obligations of the business depends on what type of entity the S corporation is under state civil law. For tax purposes it is treated very similarly to a partnership. This means that S-Corporations don't pay federal income tax but report the results of their operations to the shareholders who report their share of corporate income or loss on their personal taxes. A separate bank account and separate records are required with this form of entity. This is mostly used for small businesses and start- ups.

C-Corporation

Owners are called stock or shareholders; ownership is easily transferable; owners are taxed at the corporate and shareholder levels (double taxation); corporation is a separate entity from owners; shareholders are not personally liable for business debts; requires filing of Articles of Incorporation with the Secretary of State. S-Corporation Limited ownership; no double taxation; income or loss is passed through to the owners; requires filing of Articles of Incorporation with the Secretary of State and IRS form SS-4 (S-Election). Most major retailers use this entity structure (e.g. Target, Walmart, Home Depot, etc.)

The entire process to form any corporate entity can be done for you surprisingly quickly. Depending on what state you live in its rather inexpensive. In order to capitalize on any business financing available to you, and to separate your business and personal credit, you have to have a real corporate business entity.

Although there are some avenues and other places you can go to get up to $50K in funding without having a business entity set up – it's not always easy to get with just your business credit profile.

For a larger loan amount of $50,000 and more most banks and other lenders require you to have a minimum of one bank reference ... and an average daily balance of at least $10,000 for the past three months. This yields a "Bank Rating" of Low-5 (meaning an ADB of $5,000 to $30,000). A lower rating ... say a High-4, or balance of $7,000 to $9,999 ...however, this won't put a stop to your application. But it will slow it down.

Do whatever you can to get this minimum figure in your account ... knowing that you don't USE this money! It's only kept there to keep your Bank Rating up. Also make sure that your business bank accounts are reported exactly the way all your business records are ... with the exact same physical address (No P.O. Box or Mail Box, Etc. places) and phone number.

Make absolutely sure that every credit agency and trade credit vendor – in fact every record-keeper (financial records, income tax, web addresses and e-mail addresses, directory assistance) – also lists you the same way. No lender is going to stop to consider all the ways you might be listed, when they look into your "creditworthiness". If they can't find what they need – easily! – the bank will simply turn you down. Bankers are lazy so they will easily dismiss your file for small simple errors that may not even be your fault so it is important to constantly update and check that all your information is correct and aligned with your business loan application.

Business credit cannot, and does not, exist for a sole proprietor. All that a sole proprietor has available are personal loans or lines of credit. This credit is tied to your personal social security number.

What type of entity do you need? You'll need to consult your CPA, tax attorney, or lawyer for advice on what type of entity will fit your business best. You can be an S corporation, C corporation, LLP or limited liability company to build business credit.

#5

Maintaining Your D&B Report

Hopefully, at this point you have either went on our website, reviewed our FaceBook page, or went on our YouTube Channel and learned the proper steps to building your business credit profile. Once you have completed that and have filed your business profile with D&B creditors you can start reporting to D&B. This is a very important part because you want to make sure the vendors and lenders are reporting to D&B. When I was applying for loans and merchant services I found out a lot companies do not report to D&B. So make sure you ask a vendor or lender prior to applying. To make your job a little easier I have done some of the work for you and have included in the "Bonus Section" a few vendors that report to D&B. You can apply for these vendors with and without personal guarantees.

Your report will be set up and more than likely you will start with a high PAYDEX score (see Section #6), you'll want to be sure to maintain your report.

Check your report periodically. You may want to consider purchasing the Monitoring Service that D&B offers. This service is a little pricey but this will help your reporting credit lines quicker as oppose to you going directly to other businesses and request them to post. Or you can do it yourself and the cost is FREE through iupdate on Dun & Bradstreet. There are a lot of FREE resources on D&B that are very helpful.

D&B will assist you in updating your business credit report. This service also allows you to receive alerts, whether positive or negative, on your report. There are several areas that you will be notified of, if they change, including:

- Credit Rating
- Suits, liens or judgments on your business
- PAYDEX score changes
- Changes to financial statements
- Other significant news involving your business
- Updates on specific laws
- Credit Risk
- Other Companies Information

#6

How To Raise Your PAYDEX Score

The most important sections of your D&B Business Credit Report is the payment summary section. There are two scores in this section that are critical to the report and can separate a good report from a bad one. While the two scores – the PAYDEX score and the PAYDEX score key – are related, they deal with separate issues that you need to know and understand.

Your PAYDEX score is a statistical measure of your business creditworthiness and your ability to pay your debts. This is similar to your personal creditworthiness FICO score. A PAYDEX score of 80 is similar to that of a 700 personal FICO score. You'll need a PAYDEX score of 80 to obtain the most favorable financing. This means you pay all your bills on time. To obtain a PAYDEX score, you need at least five trade accounts reporting to your file ...

but the score itself is calculated by using as many as 875 payments.

You will also want those accounts to report favorable payment history. If you pay your bills on time, they will. If you pay your bills late, your PAYDEX score will drop. Depending on how early or late you pay your bills, your PAYDEX score will adjust accordingly. If you pay early, then you can achieve a score that is over 80. How timely you pay your bills (your PAYDEX score) is a good indicator to lenders of how likely you are to pay your bills in the future.

Lenders look at this score carefully when deciding whether or not to give you a loan. I've included a D&B PAYDEX score key chart below for your reference. Getting a PAYDEX score key of 80 means you have a perfect score. When you pay all your bills on time, meaning on or before the due date, you'll get a perfect score. Remember, to get this score, you need to have 5 trade references reporting to D&B on your company.

- 100 Anticipate
- 90 Discount
- 80 Prompt
- 70 Average
- 60 Slow to 22 Days
- 50 Slow to 30 Days
- 40 Slow to 60 Days
- 30 Slow to 90 Days
- 20 Slow to 120 Days

This can be one of the most difficult credit-building requirements to meet. Why?

Unfortunately you are at the mercy of your vendors to report to D&B. However, what is very helpful is when your vendors are also D&B reporters you can tell them it's an advantage to them when they report from their company. One of the best things you can do here is ask your suppliers for 30-day payment terms ... and ask them to report your payment history to Dun & Bradstreet.

Another important aspect of the PAYDEX system that most business owners don't know about is that the PAYDEX is a "weighted average" score ... giving more weight to the trade accounts that report higher amounts of credit extended and less weight to trade accounts that are reporting lower dollar amounts of credit.

So what does that mean to you?

If you are having any trouble "meeting all your

credit payback obligations" – in other words, if you're going to have to let any of your bills "slide" this month – be sure to pay your "largest dollar" creditors first! This way, their reporting – which carries more weight in your Paydex score – will remain positive.

However, always contact your creditors if you're not able to pay … and let them know that you're not "ignoring them". Give your creditors an actual date, if you can. From a creditor's point of view, the only thing worse than not being paid what's owed to you … is not even being told that you're not being paid!

Another area where you can benefit greatly is monitoring your vendors and scheduling out payment terms so you are not paying every vendor at the same time. When you are negotiating terms you should already have each vendor planned out of which vendor is most important as well as what vendor you utilize the most.

WARNING!!!!!!

There are "services" that promise to get this process done for you in one month. What they do is have their vendors report an excellent payment history even though you've just started with them. Don't do it! This is blatant fraud ... and they'll charge you up to $2,000 or more to provide this "service". The only way I see this being beneficial and legal is if you are actually going to utilize their vendors.

There are several vendors to choose from. You must find the right vendors, with the right products and services for your business, on credit terms that are right for you.

Another **WARNING !!!!** ... make sure the vendors you choose have the capability of reporting your payment history promptly and legally.

#7

Find Out Who is Reporting On Your Business

Many business owners find, when they receive their Business Information Report from D&B, that they have a low PAYDEX score. They scratch their heads and wonder why. After all ... they're paying their bills on time. You won't be able to find out which companies are reporting negative information to your file as D&B doesn't give businesses this information. You will, however, be able to obtain a list of all the companies that are reporting to your file. On a side not Experian does give you a more detailed updated of your Business Credit profile.

Upon request D&B, will give you an alphabetical list of all the companies reporting to the business credit bureau ...as well as the number of times they reported.

If you'd like to see this list, call your D&B representative and asked them for the list of companies reporting on your business. There must be at least five companies reporting before your Representative will be able to pull this list.

Once you get your report, turn to page 2. You'll find an overview of the companies that have reported the dollar-weighted payments ... and your PAYDEX score. The companies will be sorted by supplier industry.

If you have less than 20 companies on your list, your D&B representative might choose to simply read the list to you over the phone, or e-mail you the information. (If you don't receive the report, make sure you follow up with your Representative.)

Other information you'll find on this report includes: the total dollar amount of all trades reported to your account ... the largest amount that any one trade has reported ... and the percentage of payments that have been made to the top 10 industries.

Nearly every D&B report contains some errors, so don't be alarmed if you do review your report and find an error or two. Most problems needing resolution will be dealt with through the iUpdate website; however, any major issues will need special attention. In most cases you can call and have a D&B representative investigate the matter and take it off for free. Depending on the D&B account representative they may tell you they charge to fix the problem. This is not true. However; if you have a few issues on the report it may be beneficial to pay the service to have the error removed quickly and efficiently so that it doesn't affect your file.

Always make sure your business credit file is accurate! This is extremely important, as the

Fair Credit Reporting Act does not apply to businesses. If there is something wrong on your business credit report, or if you skip a step in setting it up, you have no legal recourse to have that information removed. If your file was set-up incorrectly, there's a good chance your business credit file could be put in the "High Risk" category, making it nearly impossible to remove inaccuracies.

Make sure you follow each step and take no short cuts. We can't stress this enough. This book – like any other you might read – is only a guide. Your own situation may vary depending on your particular situation. Therefore, your special needs to a particular situation, this book may not give you.

The Next Step

Now that you've reached this point, we know you're serious about building your business credit. But please understand the purpose of this book is not to encourage you to "go alone".

PLEASE VISIT OUR WEBSITE at healthyfinancialfutures.com OR Go to our YOUTUBE Channel at Healthy Financial Futures where you can get free access to information on how to build your business credit profile.

The business credit arena can be confusing and full of myths and scammers. You really need the help of a friendly guide who knows the way around those pitfalls ... and can take you in one side and out the other ... safely ... and profitably.

> CALL ONE OF OUR CONSULTANTS AT 888-313- 0333 TO BOOK A FREE CONSULTATION OR GO TO healthyfinancialfutures.com and sign up for a FREE CONSULTATION.

We've explained a lot, already, in this brief guide ... but there is so much more to building business credit the right way. It can't be fully explained through a book because every contingency you might run up against may be different for each business!

BONUS CHAPTER

VENDORS FOR BUILDING YOUR BUSINESS CREDIT TODAY

The most amazing thing about building business credit is utilizing the things you do everyday to build your business credit profile. In this detailed list below you will find vendors that you use on a daily basis to help build your company's credit in your company's name.

As a customer, being granted business credit is a privilege by the creditor to defer the payment of a debt over time. Like consumer credit grantors (e.g., credit card companies), business credit grantors evaluate the creditworthiness of the business to determine whether or not to issue credit. That evaluation is based heavily on the applicant's business credit score.

Establishing credit for a business is a process that should be done over time. The older your business the more options the business will have to build credit without the use of personal guarantees. So with that being said some of the vendors below should not be utilized until you have had some business credit history establish. It is my suggestion if you are just getting started to start with the following vendors or speak with one of our consultants for step-by-step instructions at Healthy Financial Futures, Inc.

- ULINE
- RELIABLE
- QUILLS

These 3 basic vendors will allow you to start building your profile immediately.

Congratulations! You're now on your way to building excellent business credit scores.

Reliable Office Supplies

www.reliable.com

Phone: 1-800-359-5000

Service Description: Reliable Office Supplies, the small business division of Office Max, has over 30,000 items available, and offers exclusive discounts and Five Star Guaranteed service. Premier program members will enjoy and column pricing on all order and access to a full line of office products, technology, furniture, paper, janitorial and break-room supplies and much more.

Reports to: D&B, Experian, Equifax (Reports after 30days)

Getting Approved:

1) Go to https://www.reliable.com/profile/loginOrRegistration.jsp?clickLink=myAccount and create an online account.

2) Purchase your item(s).

3) Once the item(s) has been purchased you will fill a credit application and a credit review will be performed.

4) Depending on what comes back from the credit review, you will be contacted and given options on what you are qualified for.

Payment Terms: Net 30

Application: Once you place your order you will receive a credit application.

Other Information: The approval process takes between 1-5 minutes. In some cases the application may need further review. If your application is approved you will receive your credit card in the mail between 7-10 business days (2 weeks). If you are not approved you will receive a letter in the mail informing you on the reasons.

ULINE

www.uline.com

Phone: 1-800-295-5510

Payment Terms: Net 30

Service Description: Uline is a distributor of janitorial, industrial, packaging and shipping materials to businesses throughout North America.

Reports to: D&B (Reports after 30 days)

Getting Approved: No application required. You simply order what your business needs online and then put your companies information; once your company information is verified your sent out your order . No personal guarantee required.

Secured Fleet One Card

www.fleetone.com

Phone: 1-800-359-7587

Service Description: The Fleet One Card can be used to pay for fuel, tires, brakes, regular maintenance, etc. Fleet One Cards are also accepted at Kroger owned grocery and convenient stores. This includes: CityMarket, Dillons, Food4Less, FredMeyer, Fry's, Hillander JayC, KingSoopers, Kroger, Owen's, PayLess, QFC, Ralph's, and Smith's

Reports to: D&B (Reports after 30 days)

Getting Approved: There will be a personal (Equifax) and business (D&B) credit check performed. Both credit scores must be 620 or better, or if below 620 there cannot be any delinquencies. The company must have an EIN (Employer Identification Number) and for a fleet a DOT (Department of Transportation) number (http://www.fmcsa.dot.gov/registration-licensing/registration-overview.htm).

Payment Terms: Net 30

Application: *Local:* https://onlineservices.secure.force.com/appl/

Other Information: No transaction fees. Will pay cash prices vs. credit prices at gas stations. $6.00 monthly for each actively used card. The applicant will find out if they are approved or not within 24 hours. If approved the applicant can expect to receive their card in 5 days, it will arrive via FedEx. If the applicant needs the card sooner, it can be sent overnight for an extra $25.00 and it can be billed to the card.

Vendors for Office Supplies, Marketing and Print

Office Max

http://www.officemax.com

Phone: 1-888-462-5870

Service Description: OfficeMax Incorporated is a leader in integrating products, solutions and services for the workplace, whether for business or at home. The OfficeMax mission is simple: We provide workplace innovation that enables our customers to work better. The company provides office supplies and paper, print and document services, technology products and solutions, and furniture to businesses and consumers. OfficeMax consumers and business customers are served by approximately 29,000 associates through OfficeMax.com

Reports to: Corporate Experian and Equifax (If the applicant wants Office Max to D&B they must request it). The initial report can take between 60-90 days, after that they report every 30 days.

Getting Approved: Credit check on company

Payment Terms: Net 25 revolving

Application:

The Office Max Business Credit Card

https://www.citicards.com/cards/

Other Information: If applying in store the approval process can take up to 5 minutes. If applying online the approval process can take up to one week and the applicant will be notified by a letter in the mail. Once approved the applicant will receive their card in the mail within 7-10 business days (2 weeks).

Home Depot

URL: www.homedepot.com

Phone: 1-866-875-5489

Service Description: The Home Depot® is the world's largest home improvement specialty retailer, with more than 2,200 retail stores in the United States (including Puerto Rico and the U.S. Virgin Islands), Canada, and Mexico.

Reports to: D&B, Experian, Equifax

Getting Approved: You must be in business for at least three years for Home Depot to NOT require a personal guarantee. Also if under 3 years in business they will pull a business credit report. They require an EIN to apply.

Payment Terms: Net 25/30 (Reports every 30

Macy's

www.macys.com

Phone: 1-877-493-9207

Service Description: Macy's, Inc. is one of the nation's premier omnichannel retailers, with fiscal 2012 sales of $27.7 billion. The company operates the Macy's and Bloomingdale's brands with about 840 stores in 45 states, the District of Columbia, Guam and Puerto Rico under the names of Macy's and Bloomingdale's; the *macys.com* and *bloomingdales.com* websites, and 12 Bloomingdale's Outlet stores. Bloomingdale's in Dubai is operated by Al Tayer Group LLC under a license agreement. Macy's, Inc.'s diverse workforce includes approximately 175,700 employees. Prior to June 1, 2007, Macy's, Inc. was known as Federated

Department Stores, Inc. The company's shares are traded under the symbol "M" on the New York Stock Exchange.

Reports to: D&B, Corporate Experian and Equifax

Getting Approved: A credit check application would need to be filled out. Fair (640-680) credit is needed. You must also have a D&B score which they will compare to your industry average to decide on approval. Banking references might also be required. No personal guarantee for corporate accounts.

Payment Terms: Net 30 (Reports every 60 days)

Application: https://www.macys.com/service/credit/applynow/creditapp.ognc?cm_sp=navigation-_-bottom_nav-_-apply_now_save

Office Depot

URL: http://www.officedepot.com/

Phone: 1-800-733-2815

Service Description: Office Depot, Inc. is a global supplier of office products and services. The company was incorporated in 1986 with the opening of our first retail store in Fort Lauderdale, Florida. In fiscal year 2012, we sold $10.7 billion of products and services to consumers and businesses of all sizes through our three business segments:

North American Retail Division, North American Business Solutions Division and International Division. Sales are processed through multiple channels, consisting of office supply stores, a contract sales force, an outbound telephone account management sales force, internet sites, direct marketing catalogs and call centers, all supported by our network of supply chain facilities and delivery operations.

Reports to: D&B, Corporate Experian and Equifax (reports every 30 days)

Getting Approved: Credit check on overall business history. They will check your business credit profile with D&B and/or Experian. If there is insufficient credit with one agency, they will check the other. Little or no business credit with either may require a personal guarantee. Even with a PG they report in business name only, except if you default on the account. Spending amount is based off credit scores.

Depending on your time in business and credit profile, they may require trade references. When you fill out the application you can choose to leave the personal guarantee field blank.

However, you will have to resubmit an application in the store or fax if you do not get approved on business credit alone.

If you do fill out the PG section they will still first check your business credit. If it is not sufficient, only then will they use the PG. After submitting online, they will notify you in writing of your approval with 7-10 business days.

Shell Fleet Card

URL: www.shell.com

Phone: 1-888-987-4355

Service Description: Shell Oil Company is the U.S. subsidiary of the Netherlands-based Royal Dutch Shell plc, the third-largest energy company worldwide; Shell Oil sells one of the most recognizable brands of gasoline in the U.S. Drawing from its oil and gas fields in California, Texas and the Gulf of Mexico, Shell Oil currently operates more than 22,000 service stations around the country.

Shell Oil also explores for, produces and markets oil, natural gas, chemicals and electricity directly to residential and small business customers.

Less prominent but fast-growing units in the company, such as Renewables and Shell Hydrogen, are cultivating lower-carbon energy sources like hydrogen fuel. Its parent company, Royal Dutch Shell, has more than 120,000 employees in over 145 countries around the world; Shell Oil's U.S. headquarters is located in Houston.

Reports to: D&B, Experian, Equifax

Getting Approved: Users have reported to D&B scores of at least 70 and Experian scores of at least 650 for approval. No personal guarantee with business credit history established. Newer businesses with no credit history can provide a personal guarantee.

Payment Terms: Net 30/Revolving

Application:

Shell Fleet Credit Card:

https://www.accountonline.com/ACQ/RPL/Web

Shell Fleet Plus Card:

https://www.accountonline.com/ACQ/RPL/Web/Apply?

Quill, Reliable, Uline, Strategic Network Solutions, Grainger, and several others should be able to give you one without a reference. Some may require that you prepay your other the first or second time, but these will work for start. Also, when I applied for my DUNS, i got mine less than a week, but if you get a call from D&B about purchasing anything, just kindly decline any offers they provide you. I would wait until you got your duns number just to have it at hand for any vendor or creditor that asks for it. Also make sure you have applied for your EIN too. You can get that free and basically instantly online.

Revolving Credit Accounts

The Starting Set of Revolving Credit Accounts

The rules for applying with revolving accounts are;

1. Always submit each application with your personally SSN information left blank.
2. If any of the revolving accounts ask for a social security number, be sure to tell them you want to first try qualifying for credit terms based solely on your business information.
3. You need to provide a personal guarantee (PG) with some of these providers. Giving a PG is OK as it only affects the guarantor's personal credit in the case of total default. A few late payments will NOT effect your personal credit, but you still should not be late on payments.

Walmart

URL: www.walmart.com

Phone: 1-800-WALMART (925-6278)

1-877-294-7548 (Walmart Credit Services)

Service Description: All of the stores in our worldwide Wal-Mart family remain committed to one mission: saving people money so they can live better. Every week, 176 million customers visit an ASDA, Mi Bodega Aurrera, Changomas, Neighborhood Market, Sam's Club, Seiyu, Superama, Wal-Mart store, Supercenter or one of our many other formats around the globe. In each of the markets where we operate, we work to leverage our strengths as a global company while meeting the local needs of customers and communities around the world.

Reports to: D&B (Every 20 days)

Getting Approved: Verifying company information (EIN, Business License, etc.) Will look at the D&B profile, years in business

Payment Terms: Net 20

Application: https://www.onlinecreditcenter4.com/EApplyCommercial/load.do?cHash=9941244770

Sears

URL: https://www.citibank.com/us/cards/srs/

Phone: 1-800-917-7700

Service Description: Sears, Roebuck and Co. hasn't outgrown the mall scene, but it's spending more time in other places. Beyond its 840 US mall-based stores, Sears has more than 1,400 other locations nationwide. These include more than 900 independently owned Sears Hometown Stores (formerly known as dealer stores) in small towns, 105 Sears hardware stores, and about 30 free-standing Sears Auto Centers. Sears' stores sell apparel, tools, and appliances (Kenmore), and provide home services (remodeling, appliance repairs) under the Sears Parts & Repair Services and A&E Factory brands. It also operates a growing online business. Sears was acquired by Kmart Holding Corp. in 2005. The deal formed Sears Holdings, which owns both chains.

Reports to: D&B, Experian and Equifax (

Getting Approved: no set score, standard credit check, no delinquencies. Sears requires a good business credit scores from D&B. If you do not have good scores with D&B, they will also check Experian and Equifax. If they determine your credit history is strong enough, then they do not require a personal guaranteed unless your business credit is exceptional. Leave the SSN area blank to try to qualify under the business name only. You will need to provide the EIN number.

Payment Terms: Net 30

Sam's Club

URL: http://www.samsclub.com/sams/pagedetails/content.jsp?pageName=082009_00004

Phone: 1-888-746-7726

Service Description: Sam's Club is an American chain of membership-only retail warehouse clubs owned and operated by Walmart Stores, Inc., founded in 1983 and named after Walmart founder Sam Walton. As of 2012[update] Sam's Club chain serves 47 million U.S and Puerto Rican members and is the 8th largest U.S. retailer. As of January 31, 2008 (2008-01-31)[update] Sam's Club ranks second in sales volume among warehouse clubs behind Costco, despite the fact that Sam's has more retail locations.

Best Buy

URL: http://www.bestbuy.com/site/Finance/Credit-Cards/pcmcat102500050032.c?id=pcmcat102500050032

Phone: 1-888-237-8289

Service Description: Best Buy is the world's largest multi-channel consumer electronics retailer with stores in the United States, Canada, China, Europe and Mexico. We are the 10th largest online retailer in the U.S. and Canada, we have the number one customer loyalty program of its kind and more than 1.6 billion visitors to our websites and stores each year. Our more than 165,000 employees are committed to helping deliver the technology solutions that provide value, enabling access to people, knowledge, ideas and fun – whether online, via mobile device or in our stores.

Reports to: Experian, Equifax, Transunion

Getting Approved: Credit check performed – Fair credit required (641-680)

Payment Terms: Net 30

Application:

https://www-ssl.bestbuy.com/site/olspage.jsp?id=pcat17094&type=page&media=L5IM014AAX1112001702XXTTX&LanguageIndicator=en

Other Information: You can apply online or in store. The process takes 5 minutes. Some applications may need further review and that process can take up to 2 weeks and the applicant will be notified of the decision via mail. If approved the applicant can expect to receive their card in 7-10 business days (2 weeks) in the mail. If the card takes longer than 2 weeks, please call customer service.

Southwest Airlines

URL: http://www.southwest.com/

Phone: 1-800-792-0001

Service Description: With 40 consecutive years of profitability, Dallas-based Southwest Airlines (NYSE: LUV) continues to differentiate itself from other carriers with exemplary Customer Service delivered by nearly 46,000 Employees to more than 100 million Customers annually. On May 2, 2011, Southwest completed the acquisition of AirTran Holdings, Inc., and now operates AirTran Airways as a wholly-owned subsidiary. Southwest is the nation's largest carrier in terms of originating domestic passengers boarded and, including AirTran, operates the largest fleet of Boeing aircraft in the world to serve 97 destinations in 41 states, the District of Columbia, the Commonwealth of Puerto Rico, and six near-international countries. Southwest has lower unit costs (adjusted for stage length), on average, than virtually all major domestic airlines and consistently has one of the best overall Customer Service records. Southwest's all-Boeing fleet consistently offers leather seating and the comfort of full-size cabins. The majority of Southwest's fleet is equipped with a new, eco-friendly cabin interior, and satellite-based WiFi connectivity, including a new in-flight entertainment portal, which gives Customers the ability to watch live TV, news, sports, and movies.

Reports to: D&B, Corporate Experian and Equifax (Reports every 30 days)

Getting Approved: Credit check on overall company history

Payment Terms: Net 30

Hawaiian Airlines

URL: www.hawaiianairlines.com

Phone: 1-800-551-0839

Service Description: Hawaiian Airlines, Inc. is the largest airline in Hawaii. It is the 11th largest commercial airline in the US, based in Honolulu, Hawaii. The airline operates its main hub at Honolulu International Airport and a secondary hub out of Kahului Airport on the island of Maui. Hawaiian Airlines is owned by Hawaiian Holdings, Inc.

Reports to: D&B, Corporate Experian and Equifax

Getting Approved: Credit check on personal credit performed. Must have fair to good credit (641-720)

Payment Terms: Net 30

Delta Airlines

URL: www.delta.com

Phone: 1-800-519-6136

Service Description: Delta Air Lines, Inc. (Delta) provides scheduled air transportation for passengers and cargo throughout the United States and around the world. The Company's route network gives it a presence in every domestic and international market. Delta's route network is centered around the hub system it operate at airports in Amsterdam, Atlanta, Cincinnati, Detroit, Memphis, Minneapolis-St. Paul, New York-JFK, Paris-Charles de Gaulle, Salt Lake City and Tokyo-Narita. Each of these hub operations includes flights that gather and distribute traffic from markets in the geographic region surrounding the hub to domestic and international cities and to other hubs. The Company's network is supported by a fleet of aircraft that is varied in terms of size and capabilities.

www.ingramcontent.com/pod-product-compliance
Lightning Source LLC
Chambersburg PA
CBHW060400190526
45169CB00002B/677